Footprints

One night I dreamed a dream.
I was walking along the beach with my Lord.
Across the dark sky flashed scenes from my life.
For each scene, I noticed two sets of footprints in the sand,
one belonging to me and one to my Lord.
When the last scene of my life shot before me
I looked back at the footprints in the sand
and to my surprise,
I noticed that many times along the path of my life
there was only one set of footprints.
I realized that this was at the lowest and saddest times of my life.
This always bothered me
and I questioned the Lord
about my dilemma.
"Lord, You told me when I decided to follow You,
You would walk and talk with me all the way.
But I'm aware that during the most troublesome times of my life
there is only one set of footprints.
I just don't understand why, when I needed You most,
You leave me."
He whispered, "My precious child,
I love you and will never leave you
never, ever, during your trials and testings.
When you saw only one set of footprints
it was then that I carried you."

—©1964 by Margaret Fishback Powers

To: _____

God is with you. He will not fail you or forsake you.

1 Chronicles 28:20

From: _____

Footprints

Copyright 1999 by Margaret Fishback Powers

ISBN 0-310-97502-6

Excerpts adapted from: Footprints: Scripture with Reflections Inspired by the Best-Loved Poem. Copyright 1998 by Margaret Fishback Powers. Published by Zondervan Publishing House.

Requests for information should be addressed to:
    Inspirio, the Gift Group of Zondervan
    Grand Rapids, Michigan 49530

Senior Editor: Gwen Ellis
Project Editor: Sarah Hupp
Designer: Pam Moore of Steve Diggs and Friends
Illustrations: Leslie Wu
Interior Layout: Laura Klynstra

Printed in China

01 02 03 04 05 /HK/ 13 12 11 10 9

Footprints

Margaret Fishback Powers

inspirio

The gift group of Zondervan

Be Thou My Vision

Be Thou my Vision, O Lord of my heart—
Nought be all else to me, save that Thou art;
Thou my best thought, by day or by night—
Waking or sleeping, Thy presence my light.

Riches I heed not, nor man's empty praise—
Thou mine inheritance, now and always;
Thou and Thou only, first in my heart—
High King of heaven, my Treasure Thou art.

High King of heaven, my victory won,
May I reach heaven's joy, O bright heav'n's Sun!
Heart of my own heart, whatever befall,
Still be my Vision, O Ruler of all.

Trans. by Mary E. Byrne; Versified by Eleanor H. Hull

God can assure us of his presence in dreams.

On my bed I remember you;
> I think of you through the watches of the night.
Because you are my help,
> I sing in the shadow of your wings.
My soul clings to you;
> your right hand upholds me.

Psalm 63:6–8

I will pour out my Spirit on all people.
Your sons and daughters will prophesy,
> your old men will dream dreams,
> your young men will see visions.

Joel 2:28

When a prophet of the LORD is among you,
> I reveal myself to him in visions,
> I speak to him in dreams.

Numbers 12:6

God can guide us with our dreams.

An angel of the Lord appeared to Joseph in a dream. "Get up," he said, "take the child and his mother and escape to Egypt. Stay there until I tell you, for Herod is going to search for the child to kill him." . . . . After Herod died, an angel of the Lord appeared in a dream to Joseph in Egypt and said, "Get up, take the child and his mother and go to the land of Israel, for those who were trying to take the child's life are dead."

Matthew 2:13, 19–20

During the night Paul had a vision of a man of Macedonia standing and begging him, "Come over to Macedonia and help us." After Paul had seen the vision, we got ready at once to leave for Macedonia, concluding that God had called us to preach the gospel to them.

Acts 16:9–10

Don't ignore your dreams. God can use our dreams to tell us something about his character or assure us of his promises. Some dreams may be about circumstances or situations we only wish would happen. These dreams very often will not come true. Yet dreams that are inspired by the Holy Spirit are different. They are worth retelling and following. When God speaks to us in such a dream, he will help us understand it. He will reassure us of his presence with us and help make those dreams come true.

Trust and Obey

When we walk with the Lord
In the light of His Word,
What a glory He sheds on our way!
While we do His good will
He abides with us still,
And with all who will trust and obey.

Then in fellowship sweet
We will sit at His feet,
Or we'll walk by His side in the way;
What He says we will do,
Where He sends we will go—
Never fear, only trust and obey.

Trust and obey—
For there's no other way
To be happy in Jesus
But to trust and obey.

John H. Sammis

I will put my dwelling place among you . . . I will walk among you and be your God, and you will be my people.

Leviticus 26:11–12

Noah was a righteous man, blameless among the people of his time, and he walked with God.

Genesis 6:9

If we claim to have fellowship with him yet walk in the darkness, we lie and do not live by the truth.

1 John 1:6

Jesus said, "I pray also for those who will believe in me . . . that all of them may be one, Father, just as you are in me and I am in you. May they also be in us so that the world may believe that you have sent me. I have given them the glory that you gave me, that they may be one as we are one: I in them and you in me."

John 17:20–23

Our fellowship is with the Father and with his Son, Jesus Christ. . . .

God is light; in him there is no darkness at all. . . .

If we walk in the light, as he is in the light, we have fellowship with one another, and the blood of Jesus, his Son, purifies us from all sin.

1 John 1:3,5,7

Those who obey his commands live in him, and he in them. And this is how we know that he lives in us: We know it by the Spirit he gave us.

1 John 3:24

"I am coming, and I will live among you," declares the LORD.

Zechariah 2:10

*J*ust as a consistent program of walking improves muscle tone and strengthens the heart, so our spiritual life will also reap benefits when we are consistent in walking with the Lord. A close walk with the Savior will ensure a sweet fellowship that will bring lasting joy, heavenly peace, and unending strength. God wants our walk with him to be a joyful, shared togetherness. Such an intimate walk of faith with the Lord will assure us of his love. Our close fellowship with him will help us cross the rough places on our journey home without the slightest care.

Across the dark

sky flashed scenes

from my life.

O Love That Will Not Let Me Go

O Love that will not let me go,
I rest my weary soul in Thee;
I give Thee back the life I owe,
That in Thine ocean depths its flow
  May richer, fuller be.
O Light that followest all my way,
I yield my flick'ring torch to Thee;
My heart restores its borrowed ray,
That in Thy sunshine's blaze its day
  May brighter, fairer be.
O Joy that seekest me thru pain,
I cannot close my heart to Thee;
I trace the rainbow thru the rain,
And feel the promise is not vain
  That morn shall tearless be.

George Matheson

Find rest, O my soul, in God alone;

my hope comes from him.

He alone is my rock and my salvation;

he is my fortress, I will not be shaken.

My salvation and my honor depend on God;

he is my mighty rock, my refuge.

Psalm 62:5–7

Jesus said, "Do not let your hearts be troubled.

Trust in God; trust also in me."

John 14:1

Surely God is my salvation;

I will trust and not be afraid.

The LORD, the LORD, is my strength and my song;

he has become my salvation.

Isaiah 12:2

Those who hope in the LORD
will renew their strength.
They will soar on wings like eagles;
they will run and not grow weary,
they will walk and not be faint.

Isaiah 40:31

Blessed is the man
who does not walk in the counsel of the wicked
or stand in the way of sinners
or sit in the seat of mockers.
But his delight is in the law of the LORD,
and on his law he meditates day and night. . . .
Whatever he does prospers.

Psalm 1:1–3

Because of the tender mercy of our God . . .
the rising sun will come to us from heaven
to shine on those living in darkness
and in the shadow of death,
to guide our feet into the path of peace.

Luke 1:78–79

*I*f we live with an attitude that looks back over our lives with regrets, we are only robbing ourselves of God's mercy and assurance. God is the God of grace and hope. With God's perspective, we can trace his hand on our lives and see that he has transformed the bad things to good, just as he promised he would. As we face the uncertainties that today may bring, we have the assurance that God knows what we are facing. He is in touch with what is happening to us, and he is concerned. We can choose to live above regrets and live instead in God's peace and joy.

For each scene, I noticed two sets of footprints in the sand, one belonging to me and one to my Lord.

I've Found a Friend

I've found a Friend, O such a friend!
He loved me ere I knew Him;
He drew me with the cords of love,
And thus He bound me to Him.
And round my heart still closely twine
Those ties which naught can sever,
For I am his and he is mine,
Forever and forever.

I've found a friend, O such a friend!
He bled, He died to save me;
And not alone the gift of life,
But His own self He gave me.
Naught that I have my own I call,
I hold it for the Giver:
My heart, my strength, my life, my all
Are His and His forever.

I've found a Friend, O such a Friend!
So kind and true and tender,
So wise a Counsellor and Guide,
So mighty a Defender!
From Him who loves me now so well,
What pow'r my soul can sever?
Shall life or death or earth or hell?
No—I am his forever

Though I walk in the midst of trouble,

you preserve my life;

you stretch out your hand against the anger of my foes,

with your right hand you save me.

The LORD will fulfill his purpose for me;

your love, O LORD, endures forever—

do not abandon the works of your hands.

Psalm 138:7–8

"Because he loves me," says the LORD, "I will rescue him;

I will protect him, for he acknowledges my name.

He will call upon me, and I will answer him;

I will be with him in trouble,

I will deliver him and honor him.

With long life will I satisfy him

and show him my salvation."

Psalm 91:14–16

Where can I go from your Spirit?

     Where can I flee from your presence?

If I go up to the heavens, you are there;

     if I make my bed in the depths, you are there.

If I rise on the wings of the dawn,

     if I settle on the far side of the sea,

even there your hand will guide me,

     your right hand will hold me fast.

If I say, "Surely the darkness will hide me

     and the light become night around me,"

even the darkness will not be dark to you;

     the night will shine like the day,

     for darkness is as light to you.

Psalm 139:7–12

*T*he Lord enjoys walking with us as our companion on life's pathway. When we walk closely with him, his presence encourages us and warms our hearts. He is our strong provider, and he is in control of every aspect of our lives. He has promised never to leave us. He will provide for our every need. And he is stronger than any obstacle we may face, yet gentle enough to enfold us in his loving embrace. As God speaks his words of peace and blessing to our hearts, we can walk the path he has placed before us with assurance and joy.

When the last scene
of my life shot
before me I looked
back at the footprints
in the sand.

I Have Decided to Follow Jesus

I have decided to follow Jesus,
I have decided to follow Jesus,
No turning back, no turning back.
Tho no one join me, still I will follow,
Tho no one join me, still I will follow,
No turning back, no turning back.
The world behind me, the cross before me,
The world behind me, the cross before me,
No turning back, no turning back.

Attributed to an Indian prince

My heart is steadfast, O God;

I will sing and make music with all my soul.

Psalm 108:1

We fix our eyes not on what is seen, but on what is unseen.

For what is seen is temporary, but what is unseen is eternal.

2 Corinthians 4:18

Since we are surrounded by such a great cloud of witnesses, let us throw off everything that hinders and the sin that so easily entangles, and let us run with perseverance the race marked out for us. Let us fix our eyes on Jesus, the author and perfecter of our faith, who for the joy set before him endured the cross, scorning its shame, and sat down at the right hand of the throne of God. Consider him who endured such opposition from sinful men, so that you will not grow weary and lose heart.

Hebrews 12:1–3

God is greater than our hearts, and he knows everything.

1 John 3:20

I have fought the good fight, I have finished the race, I have kept the faith. Now there is in store for me the crown of righteousness, which the Lord, the righteous Judge, will award to me on that day—and not only to me, but also to all who have longed for his appearing.

2 Timothy 4:7–8

Let us live up to what we have already attained.

Philippians 3:16

Though you have not seen him, you love him; and even though you do not see him now, you believe in him and are filled with an inexpressible and glorious joy, for you are receiving the goal of your faith, the salvation of your souls.

1 Peter 1:8–9

*I*n Luke 9:62 Jesus reminded his listeners that there are consequences to looking back, to wishing things had been different. Whenever we look back over our lives, we need to do so with God's perspective rather than with an attitude of regret or "if only." We do not need to live a life of regrets. We can live with a forward-looking hope of glory! Though it may sometimes seem that things are out of control, we can always take comfort in God's enduring promises and constant presence. We can stand firm in the work of the Lord and live the life God offers us—a life free of regrets and full of joy.

Abide with Me

Abide with me—fast falls the eventide,

The darkness deepens—Lord, with me abide;

When other helpers fail and comforts flee,

Help of the helpless, O abide with me!

I need Thy presence ev'ry passing hour—

What but Thy grace can foil the tempter's pow'r?

Who like Thyself my guide and stay can be?

Thru cloud and sunshine, O abide with me!

Hold Thou Thy word before my closing eyes,

Shine thru the gloom and point me to the skies;

Heav'n's morning breaks and earth's vain shadows flee—

In life, in death, O Lord, abide with me!

Henry F. Lyte

He who dwells in the shelter of the Most High
will rest in the shadow of the Almighty.
I will say of the LORD, "He is my refuge and my fortress,
my God, in whom I trust."
Surely he will save you from the fowler's snare
and from the deadly pestilence.
He will cover you with his feathers,
and under his wings you will find refuge;
his faithfulness will be your shield and rampart.
If you make the Most High your dwelling—
even the LORD, who is my refuge—
then no harm will befall you,
no disaster will come near your tent.
For he will command his angels concerning you
to guard you in all your ways;
they will lift you up in their hands,
so that you will not strike your foot against a stone.

Psalm 91:1–4,9–12

"Though the mountains be shaken
    and the hills be removed,
yet my unfailing love for you will not be shaken
    nor my covenant of peace be removed,"
says the LORD, who has compassion on you. . . .
    "All your sons will be taught by the LORD,
and great will be your children's peace.
    In righteousness you will be established:
Tyranny will be far from you;
    you will have nothing to fear.
Terror will be far removed;
    it will not come near you. . . .
No weapon forged against you will prevail,
    and you will refute every tongue that accuses you.
This is the heritage of the servants of the LORD,
    and this is their vindication from me,"
declares the LORD.

Isaiah 54:10, 13–14, 17

*T*he journey of life can sometimes be very troubling. We often stumble and have difficulty following in God's footsteps. But we must never doubt God's presence with us. God will never let us down. He promises us his strength, his peace, his comfort, and his presence. When it seems that life is whirling out of control, we can take comfort in God's sovereignty and power. All we need to do is come to him with our seeking hearts and know that we can depend on him. We can never break God's promises by leaning on them.

I realized that this was at the lowest and saddest times of my life.

Come, Ye Disconsolate

Come, ye disconsolate, where'er ye languish—
Come to the mercy seat, fervently kneel;
Here bring your wounded hearts, here tell your anguish:
Earth has no sorrow that heav'n cannot heal.

Joy of the desolate, light of the straying,
Hope of the penitent, fadeless and pure!
Here speaks the Comforter, tenderly saying,
"Earth has no sorrow that heav'n cannot cure."

Here see the Bread of Life, see waters flowing
Forth from the throne of God, pure from above;
Come to the feast of love—come ever knowing
Earth has no sorrow but heav'n can remove.

Stanzas 1, 2 Thomas Moore; Stanza 3 Thomas Hastings

Praise be to the God and Father of our Lord Jesus Christ, the Father of compassion and the God of all comfort, who comforts us in all our troubles, so that we can comfort those in any trouble with the comfort we ourselves have received from God. For just as the sufferings of Christ flow over into our lives, so also through Christ our comfort overflows.

2 Corinthians 1:3–5

Jesus said, "Come to me, all you who are weary and burdened, and I will give you rest. Take my yoke upon you and learn from me, for I am gentle and humble in heart, and you will find rest for your souls."

Matthew 11:28–29

You are enthroned as the Holy One:
    you are the praise of Israel.
In you our fathers put their trust;
    they trusted you and you delivered them.
They cried to you and were saved;
    in you they trusted and were not disappointed.

Psalm 22:3–5

I remember my affliction and my wandering,

the bitterness and the gall.

I well remember them,

and my soul is downcast within me.

Yet this I call to mind

and therefore I have hope:

Because of the LORD's great love we are not consumed,

for his compassions never fail.

They are new every morning;

great is your faithfulness.

I say to myself, "The LORD is my portion;

therefore I will wait for him."

The LORD is good to those whose hope is in him,

to the one who seeks him.

Lamentations 3:19–25

I will strengthen you and help you;

I will uphold you with my righteous right hand.

Isaiah 41:10

Sorrow may cause us to doubt God's plan. Yet God reminds us that he is aware of everything that is happening to us. No sorrow is too deep that God cannot feel it with us. Whatever the circumstances, he has everything under control. And he will work his will in every circumstance. Whenever we hit rock bottom, we can rest assured of God's love and care. He hears our heartfelt cries. His encouragement can breathe new possibilities into our impossible situations. And he will answer our prayers in ways that will fill us with joy and amazement.

This always bothered me and I questioned the Lord about my dilemma.

Does Jesus Care?

Does Jesus care when my heart is pained
Too deeply for mirth and song;
As the burdens press, and the cares distress,
And the way grows weary and long?

Does Jesus care when my way is dark
With a nameless dread and fear?
As the daylight fades into deep night shades,
Does He care enough to be near?

Does Jesus care when I've said goodbye
To the dearest on earth to me,
And my sad heart aches till it nearly breaks—
Is it aught to Him? Does He see?

O yes, He cares—I know he cares!
His heart is touched with my grief;
When the days are weary, the long nights dreary,
I know my Savior cares.

Frank E. Graeff

Delight yourself in the LORD
  and he will give you the desires of your heart.

Commit your way to the LORD;
  trust in him and he will do this:
He will make your righteousness shine like the dawn,
  the justice of your cause like the noonday sun.

Psalm 37:4–6

Blessed is the man who trusts in the LORD,
  whose confidence is in him.
He will be like a tree planted by the water
  that sends out its roots by the stream.
It does not fear when heat comes;
  its leaves are always green.
It has no worries in a year of drought
  and never fails to bear fruit.

Jeremiah 17:7–8

The LORD is good,

a refuge in times of trouble.

He cares for those who trust in him.

Nahum 1:7

Cast all your anxiety on him because he cares for you.

1 Peter 5:7

The LORD himself goes before you and will be with you; he will never leave you nor forsake you.

Deuteronomy 31:8

"I know the plans I have for you," declares the LORD, "plans to prosper you and not to harm you, plans to give you hope and a future."

Jeremiah 29:11

Trust in the LORD with all your heart

    and lean not on your own understanding;

in all your ways acknowledge him,

    and he will make your paths straight.

Proverbs 3:5–6

Show me your ways, O LORD,

    teach me your paths;

guide me in your truth and teach me,

    for you are God my Savior,

    and my hope is in you all day long.

Remember, O LORD, your great mercy and love,

    for they are from of old.

Psalm 25:4–6

Let us acknowledge the LORD;

    let us press on to acknowledge him.

As surely as the sun rises,

    he will appear;

he will come to us like the winter rains,

    like the spring rains that water the earth.

Hosea 6:3

Glorify the LORD with me;

let us exalt his name together.

I sought the LORD, and he answered me;

he delivered me from all my fears.

Those who look to him are radiant;

their faces are never covered with shame.

This poor man called, and the LORD heard him;

he saved him out of all his troubles.

The angel of the LORD encamps around those who fear him,

and he delivers them.

Taste and see that the LORD is good;

blessed is the man who takes refuge in him.

Fear the LORD, you his saints,

for those who fear him lack nothing.

The lions may grow weak and hungry,

but those who seek the LORD lack no good thing.

Psalm 34:3–10

When the outlook is not good, we don't need to fret or worry. Fretting will only tie us in knots. Worry will only cast a big shadow over small problems—a shadow that should never cross our lives. We need to realize that God sees tomorrow more clearly than we see yesterday or today. The future is completely in his hands. We must trust that the Lord will take our faith, limited as it may be, and make it into something of lasting value. We need to get our arms around God's wisdom, remember his faithfulness, and depend upon his grace. Whatever our questions, whatever our circumstances, God is still in control. He will give us the answer we seek.

"Lord, You told me when I decided to follow You, You would walk and talk with me all the way."

All the Way My Savior Leads Me

All the way my Savior leads me—
What have I to ask beside?
Can I doubt His tender mercy,
Who thru life has been my Guide?
Heav'nly peace, divinest comfort,
Here by faith in Him to dwell!
For I know, whate'er befall me,
Jesus doeth all things well.

All the way my Savior leads me—
Cheers each winding path I tread,
Gives me grace for ev'ry trial,
Feeds me with the living bread.
Tho my weary steps may falter
And my soul athirst may be,
Gushing from the Rock before me,
Lo! A spring of joy I see.

Fanny Crosby

God has said,

"Never will I leave you;

never will I forsake you."

So we say with confidence,

"The Lord is my helper; I will not be afraid.

What can man do to me?"

Hebrews 13:5–6

The LORD is the everlasting God,

the Creator of the ends of the earth.

He will not grow tired or weary,

and his understanding no one can fathom.

He gives strength to the weary

and increases the power of the weak.

Even youths grow tired and weary,

and young men stumble and fall;

but those who hope in the LORD

will renew their strength.

They will soar on wings like eagles;

they will run and not grow weary,

they will walk and not be faint.

Isaiah 40:28–31

The LORD is my shepherd, I shall not be in want.

He makes me lie down in green pastures,

he leads me beside quiet waters,

he restores my soul.

He guides me in paths of righteousness

for his name's sake.

Even though I walk

through the valley of the shadow of death,

I will fear no evil,

for you are with me;

your rod and your staff,

they comfort me.

You prepare a table before me

in the presence of my enemies.

You anoint my head with oil;

my cup overflows.

Surely goodness and love will follow me

all the days of my life,

and I will dwell in the house of the LORD

forever.

Psalm 23

One thing I ask of the LORD,

this is what I seek:

that I may dwell in the house of the LORD

all the days of my life,

to gaze upon the beauty of the LORD

and to seek him in his temple.

For in the day of trouble

he will keep me safe in his dwelling;

he will hide me in the shelter of his tabernacle

and set me high upon a rock.

Psalm 27:4–5

No one will be able to stand up against you all the days of your life. As I was with Moses, so I will be with you; I will never leave you nor forsake you.

Joshua 1:5

Who is wise? He will realize these things.

　　Who is discerning? He will understand them.

The ways of the LORD are right;

　　the righteous walk in them,

　　but the rebellious stumble in them.

Hosea 14:9

O LORD, you have searched me

　　and you know me.

You know when I sit and when I rise;

　　you perceive my thoughts from afar.

You discern my going out and my lying down;

　　you are familiar with all my ways.

Before a word is on my tongue

　　you know it completely, O Lord.

You hem me in—behind and before;

　　you have laid your hand upon me.

Psalm 139:1–5

Decisions, decisions, decisions. It sometimes seems that all we do is make decisions. Some decisions may be simple; others may be complex. Yet sometimes the right choice may be obscure. We need someone to help tell us what to do. When we face decisions of all kinds, we should make sure to predicate our choices on our decision to follow the Lord. He will show us how to follow in his steps. Following the Lord means living your life the way he wants you to, yielding to his control in every situation. When we consistently walk with the Lord, we will find clear direction, joyful hearts, and the assurance of God's presence in every circumstance.

"During the most troublesome times of my life there is only one set of footprints."

Moment by Moment

Never a trial that He is not there,
Never a burden that He doth not bear;
Never a sorrow that He doth not share—
Moment by moment, I'm under His care.
Never a heartache and never a groan,
Never a teardrop and never a moan,
Never a danger but there on the throne,
Moment by moment, He thinks of His own.
Never a weakness that He doth not feel,
Never a sickness that He cannot heal;
Moment by moment, in woe or in weal,
Jesus, my Savior, abide with me still.
Moment by moment I'm kept in His love,
Moment by moment I've life from above;
Looking to Jesus till glory doth shine,
Moment by moment, O Lord, I am Thine.

Daniel W. Whittle

I will praise the LORD all my life;

I will sing praise to my God as long as I live.

Do not put your trust in princes,

in mortal men, who cannot save. . . .

Blessed is he whose help is the God of Jacob,

whose hope is in the LORD his God,

the Maker of heaven and earth,

the sea, and everything in them—

the LORD, who remains faithful forever.

Psalm 146:2–3, 5–6

Cast your cares on the LORD
and he will sustain you;
he will never let the righteous fall.

Psalm 55:22

If the LORD delights in a man's way,

he makes his steps firm;

though he stumble, he will not fall,

for the LORD upholds him with his hand.

I was young and now I am old,

yet I have never seen the righteous forsaken

or their children begging bread. . . .

For the LORD loves the just

and will not forsake his faithful ones.

They will be protected forever.

Psalm 37:23–25, 28

I took you from the ends of the earth,

from its farthest corners I called you.

I said, "You are my servant";

I have chosen you and have not rejected you.

So do not fear, for I am with you;

do not be dismayed, for I am your God.

I will strengthen you and help you;

I will uphold you with my righteous right hand.

Isaiah 41:9–10

This is what the LORD says . . .

"Fear not, for I have redeemed you;

I have summoned you by name; you are mine.

When you pass through the waters,

I will be with you;

and when you pass through the rivers,

they will not sweep over you.

When you walk through the fire,

you will not be burned;

the flames will not set you ablaze."

Isaiah 43:1–2

You are my hiding place;

you will protect me from trouble

and surround me with songs of deliverance.

I will instruct you and teach you in the way you should go;

I will counsel you and watch over you.

Psalm 32:7–8

The LORD says,

"He will call upon me, and I will answer him;

I will be with him in trouble,

I will deliver him and honor him.

With long life will I satisfy him

and show him my salvation."

Psalm 91:15–16

Jesus said, "Obey everything I have commanded you.

And surely I am with you always, to the very end of the age."

Matthew 28:20

I will sing of your strength,

in the morning I will sing of your love;

for you are my fortress,

my refuge in times of trouble.

O my Strength, I sing praise to you;

you, O God, are my fortress, my loving God.

Psalm 59:16–17

*T*here are times in life when we feel bereft, abandoned, alone. When loneliness overtakes us, we must remember that *we are never alone*. We can take comfort in God's promises to be with us—in our joy and in our pain, in the good times and in the bad times. God has promised that he will never forsake us. His steadfast love and faithfulness are promises we can cling to, promises that can bring us joy whenever we face the pangs of loneliness. Let us lean on these promises and receive God's peace. Let us walk in his footsteps and sense his strength. Let us stand in his presence and feel his love.

"I just don't understand why, when I needed You most, You leave me."

Never Alone

I've seen the lightning flashing
And heard the thunder roll,
I've felt sin's breakers dashing,
Which tried to conquer my soul;
I've heard the voice of my Savior,
He bid me still fight on—
He promised never to leave me,
Never to leave me alone.
No, never alone, no, never alone—
He promised never to leave me,
Never to leave me alone;
No, never alone, no, never alone—
He promised never to leave me,
Never to leave me alone.

Source unknown, nineteenth century

Seek the LORD while he may be found;

call on him while he is near.

Let the wicked forsake his way

and the evil man his thoughts.

Let him turn to the LORD, and he will have mercy on him,

and to our God, for he will freely pardon.

"For my thoughts are not your thoughts,

neither are your ways my ways,"

declares the LORD.

"As the heavens are higher than the earth,

so are my ways higher than your ways

and my thoughts than your thoughts."

Isaiah 55:6–9

I will never stop doing good to them, and I will inspire them to fear me, so that they will
never turn away from me. I will rejoice in doing them good and will assuredly plant them
in this land with all my heart and soul

Jeremiah 32:40–41

I called on your name, O LORD,
from the depths of the pit.
You heard my plea: "Do not close your ears
to my cry for relief."
You came near when I called you,
and you said, "Do not fear."
O Lord, you took up my case;
you redeemed my life.

Lamentations 3:55–58

Jesus said,
"Blessed are the poor in spirit,
for theirs is the kingdom of heaven.
Blessed are those who mourn,
for they will be comforted.
Blessed are the meek,
for they will inherit the earth.
Blessed are those who hunger and thirst for righteousness,
for they will be filled.
Blessed are the merciful,
for they will be shown mercy.
Blessed are the pure in heart,
for they will see God.
Blessed are the peacemakers,
for they will be called sons of God.

Matthew 5:3–9

When faced with bewildering circumstances, we may be tempted to ask, "Why?" But a better question to ask is, "*What* do you have in mind now, Lord?" God always has a plan. God always has a purpose in every situation for those who follow in his footsteps. When we experience God's forgiveness, we are new creatures. God's presence is with us to help us, even when we don't realize it. There is hope. There is light in the darkness. Jesus Christ, God's Son, can strengthen our faith if we will wait patiently and trust God's desire to make us more like himself. We must put away all doubts. Cast out all confusion. Then we will find a renewed faith as we follow in his footsteps.

God Leads Us Along

In shady, green pastures, so rich and so sweet,
God leads His dear children along;
Where the water's cool flow bathes the weary one's feet,
God leads His dear children along.
Sometimes on the mount where the sun shines so bright,
God leads His dear children along;
Sometimes in the valley, in darkest of night,
God leads His dear children along.
Some thru the waters, some thru the flood,
Some thru the fire, but all thru the blood;
Some thru great sorrow, but God gives a song,
In the night season and all the day long.
Tho sorrows befall us and Satan oppose,
God leads His dear children along;
Thru grace we can conquer, defeat all our foes,
God leads His dear children along.

G. A. Young, nineteenth century

How great is the love the Father has lavished on us, that we should be called children of God! And that is what we are!   .   .   .   Now we are children of God, and what we will be has not yet been made known. But we know that when he appears, we shall be like him, for we shall see him as he is.

1 John 3:1–2

Those who are led by the Spirit of God are sons of God.   .   .   .   You received the Spirit of sonship. And by him we cry, *"Abba,* Father." The Spirit himself testifies with our spirit that we are God's children. Now if we are children,then we are heirs—heirs of God and co-heirs with Christ.

Romans 8:14–17

O LORD, you are our Father.
We are the clay, you are the potter;
we are all the work of your hand.

Isaiah 64:8

I will pour water on the thirsty land,

    and streams on the dry ground;

I will pour out my Spirit on your offspring,

    and my blessing on your descendants. . . .

One will say, "I belong to the LORD";

    another will call himself by the name of Jacob;

still another will write on his hand, "The LORD's."

Isaiah 44:3, 5

What agreement is there between the temple of God and idols?
For we are the temple of the living God. As God has said: "I will live with them
and walk among them, and I will be their God and they will be my people."

    "Therefore come out from them

    and be separate,

                      says the Lord.

Touch no unclean thing,

    and I will receive you."

"I will be a Father to you,

    and you will be my sons and daughters,

             says the Lord Almighty."

2 Corinthians 6:16–18

*T*he Creator of the universe calls us his children—
what a blessing! What a privilege! What a responsibility! As children of God, we can trust that he will
provide for us. We have the assurance that he created
us and knows us by name. God also bestows on us
certain rights, privileges, and responsibilities as his
heirs. Scripture reassures us that our loving heavenly
Father will care for us just as a shepherd cares for
his sheep. And as his children, our responsibility
is to listen carefully to his voice and obey.

"I love you and will never leave you never, ever, during your trials and testings."

Day by Day

Day by day and with each passing moment,
Strength I find to meet my trials here;
Trusting in my Father's wise bestowment,
I've no cause for worry or for fear.
He whose heart is kind beyond all measure
Gives unto each day what he deems best—
Lovingly, its part of pain and pleasure,
Mingling toil with peace and rest.
"As thy days, thy strength shall be in measure,"
This the pledge to me he made.
Help me then in ev'ry tribulation
So to trust thy promises, O Lord,
That I lose not faith's sweet consolation
Offered me within thy holy word.
Help me, Lord, when toil and trouble meeting,
E'er to take, as from a father's hand,
One by one, the day, the moments fleeting,
Till I reach the promised land.

Lina Sandell Berg, trans. by Andrew L. Skoog

I am always with you;

  you hold me by my right hand.

You guide me with your counsel,

  and afterward you will take me into glory.

Whom have I in heaven but you?

  And earth has nothing I desire besides you.

My flesh and my heart may fail,

  but God is the strength of my heart

  and my portion forever.

Psalm 73:23–26

The LORD is close to the brokenhearted

  and saves those who are crushed in spirit.

Psalm 34:18

Do not be anxious about anything, but in everything, by prayer and petition, with thanksgiving, present your requests to God. And the peace of God, which transcends all understanding, will guard your hearts and your minds in Christ Jesus.

Philippians 4:6–7

I lift up my eyes to the hills—
　　where does my help come from?
My help comes from the LORD,
　　the Maker of heaven and earth.

He will not let your foot slip—
　　he who watches over you will not slumber;
indeed, he who watches over Israel
　　will neither slumber nor sleep.

The LORD watches over you—
　　the LORD is your shade at your right hand;
the sun will not harm you by day,
　　nor the moon by night.

The LORD will keep you from all harm—
　　he will watch over your life;
the LORD will watch over your coming and going
　　both now and forevermore.

Psalm 121

*T*hough we may face trouble and difficulties, sadness and pain, God is still in control, and he is always with us. When trouble rages, we must listen closely to God's voice. When the agonies of life begin to bear down upon us, God has not moved away from us. We may have moved away from him. We must return to him in faith and call on him for his strength. He wants to bring us his divine comfort. Though things may seem hopeless, no trial is so great that God cannot deliver us, no pain is so great that he cannot bring us comfort, no circumstance is ever without God's presence. When God promises never to leave us, he means just that. He is in control.

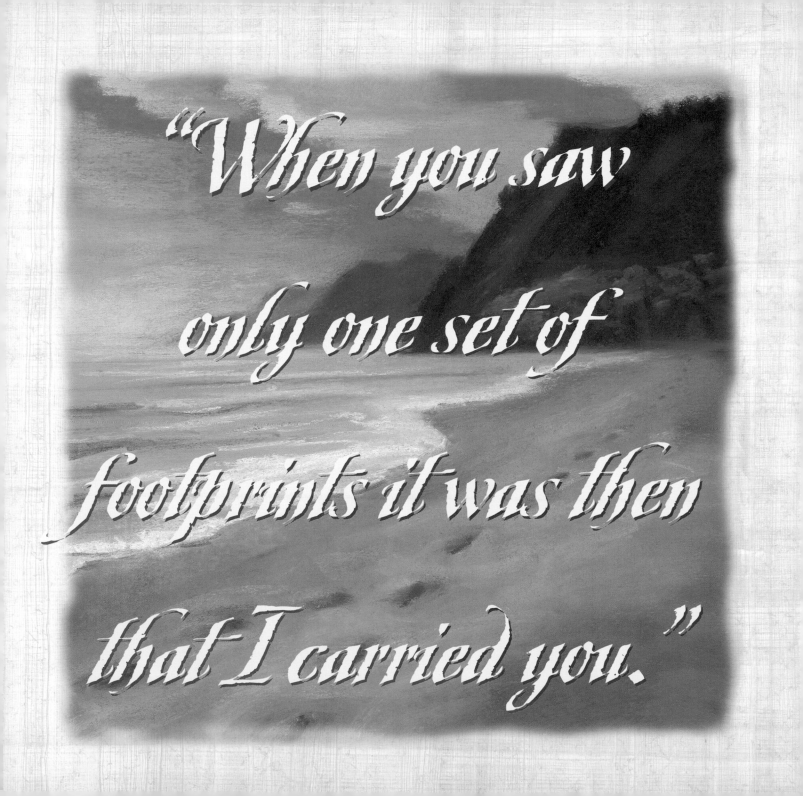

"When you saw only one set of footprints it was then that I carried you."

Leaning on the Everlasting Arms

What a fellowship, what a joy divine,
Leaning on the everlasting arms;
What a blessedness, what a peace is mine,
Leaning on the everlasting arms.
Oh, how sweet to walk in this pilgrim way,
Leaning on the everlasting arms;
Oh, how bright the path grows from day to day,
Leaning on the everlasting arms.
What have I to dread, what have I to fear,
Leaning on the everlasting arms;
I have blessed peace with my Lord so near,
Leaning on the everlasting arms.
Leaning, leaning,
Safe and secure from all alarms;
Leaning, leaning,
Leaning on the everlasting arms.

Elisha A. Hoffman

The eternal God is your refuge,

and underneath are the everlasting arms.

Deuteronomy 33:27

See, the Sovereign LORD comes with power,

and his arm rules for him.

See, his reward is with him,

and his recompense accompanies him.

He tends his flock like a shepherd:

He gathers the lambs in his arms

and carries them close to his heart.

Isaiah 40:10–11

The LORD is the strength of his people,

a fortress of salvation for his anointed one.

Psalm 28:8

He tends his flock like a shepherd:

He gathers the lambs in his arms

and carries them close to his heart;

he gently leads those that have young.

Isaiah 40:11

Cast all your anxiety on him because he cares for you.

1 Peter 5:7

The Lord has established his throne in heaven,

and his kingdom rules over all.

Praise the Lord, you his angels,

you mighty ones who do his bidding,

who obey his word.

Praise the Lord, all his heavenly hosts,

you his servants who do his will.

Praise the Lord, all his works

everywhere in his dominion.

Praise the Lord, O my soul.

Psalm 103:19–22